The Nearly Perfect Coloring Book
For the Detail Oriented

A.F. Miller

ISBN: 1517134366
ISBN-13: 978-1517134365

Tips and Tricks

Tear out this page.

Put it underneath the page you are coloring to prevent marker bleed.

Use it to test your markers and colored pencils.

Doodle in big spaces and in the margins!

Color a page with only greys.

Color a page with only browns.

Color a page with peacock colors.

Ignore the lines.

See how few colors you can use, but don't let any color touch itself.

The illustrations alternate between harder and easier.

Tear apart the book and frame your work.

Send me pictures of your colored pages!

@ashleyfmiller on Twitter

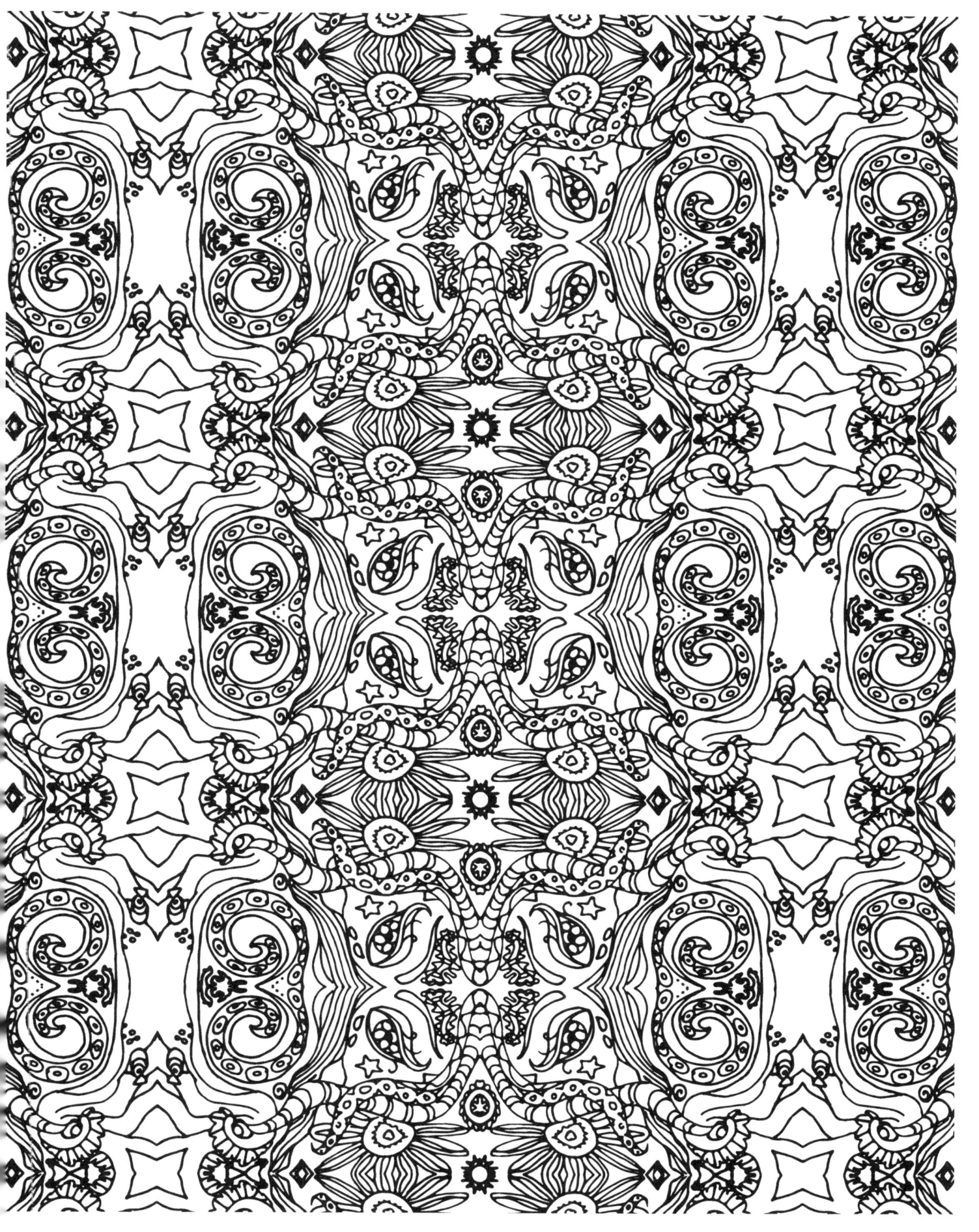

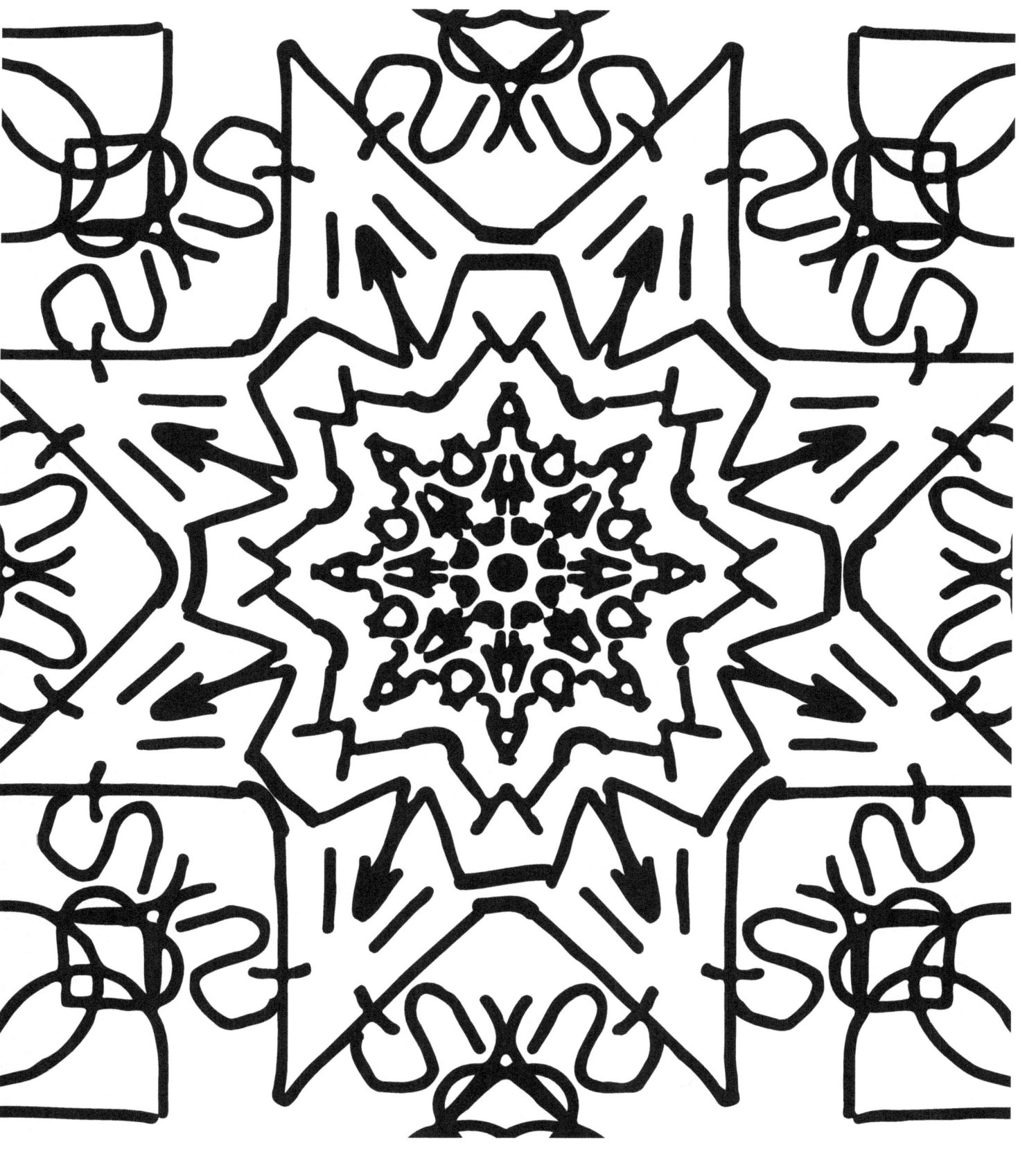

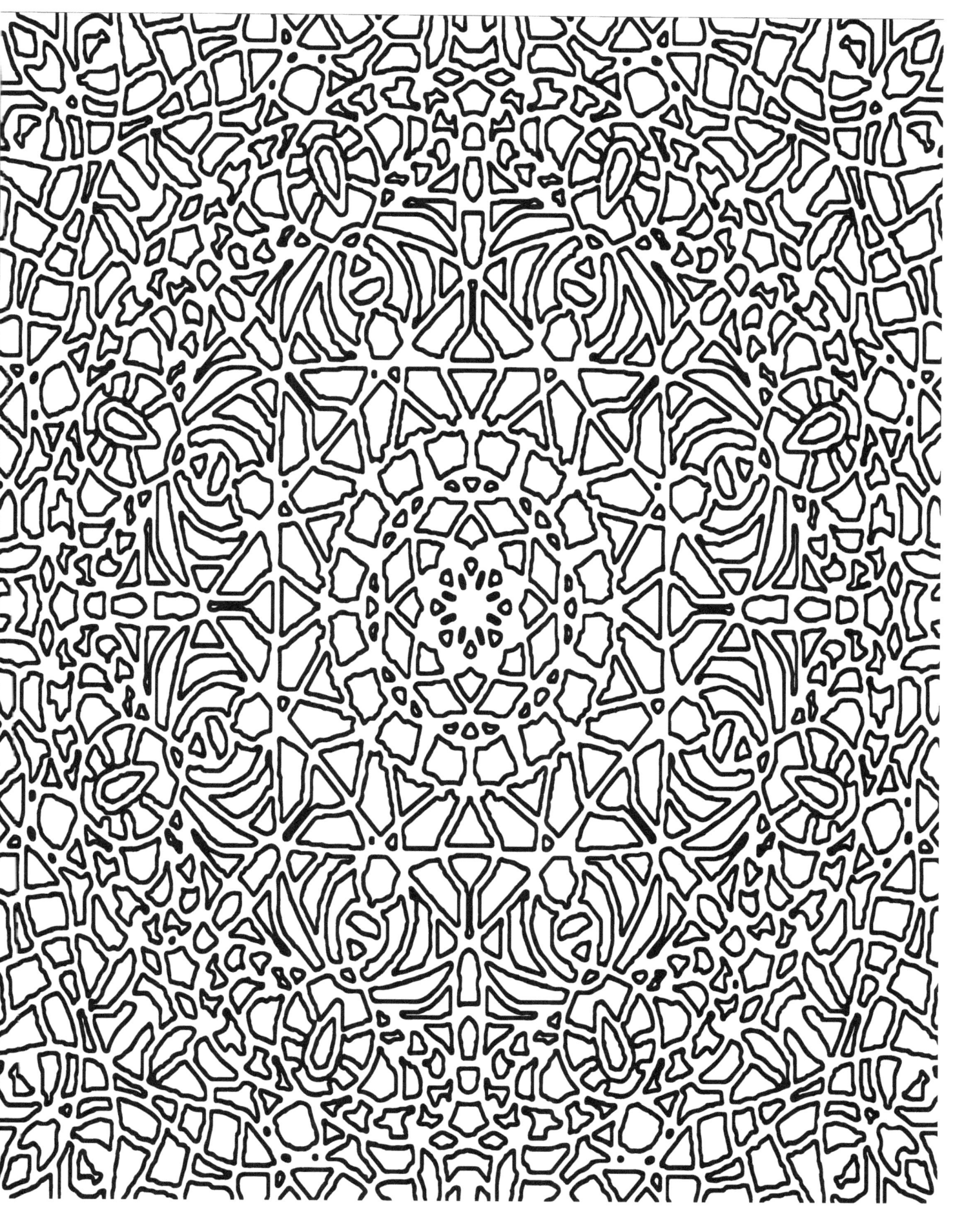

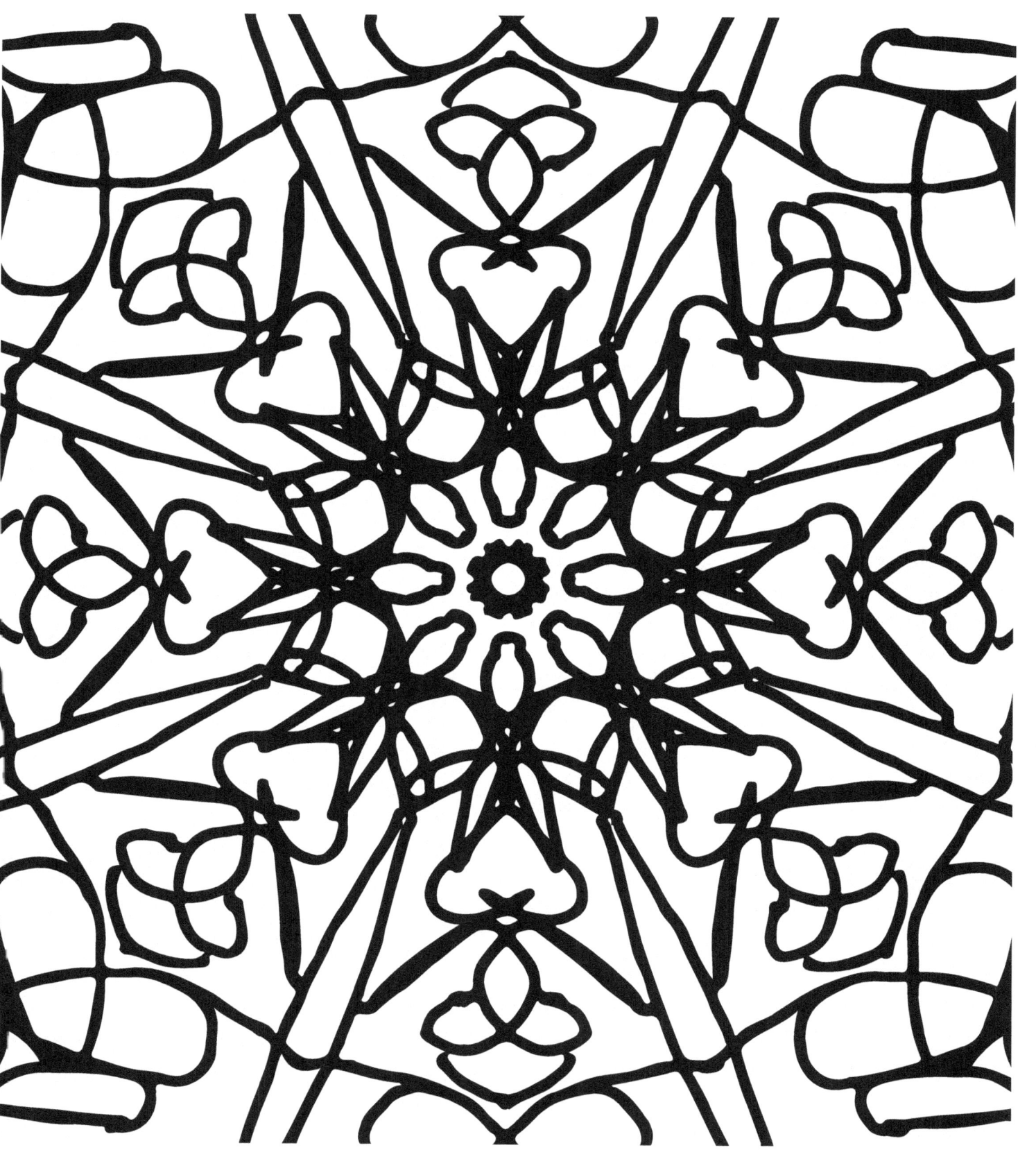

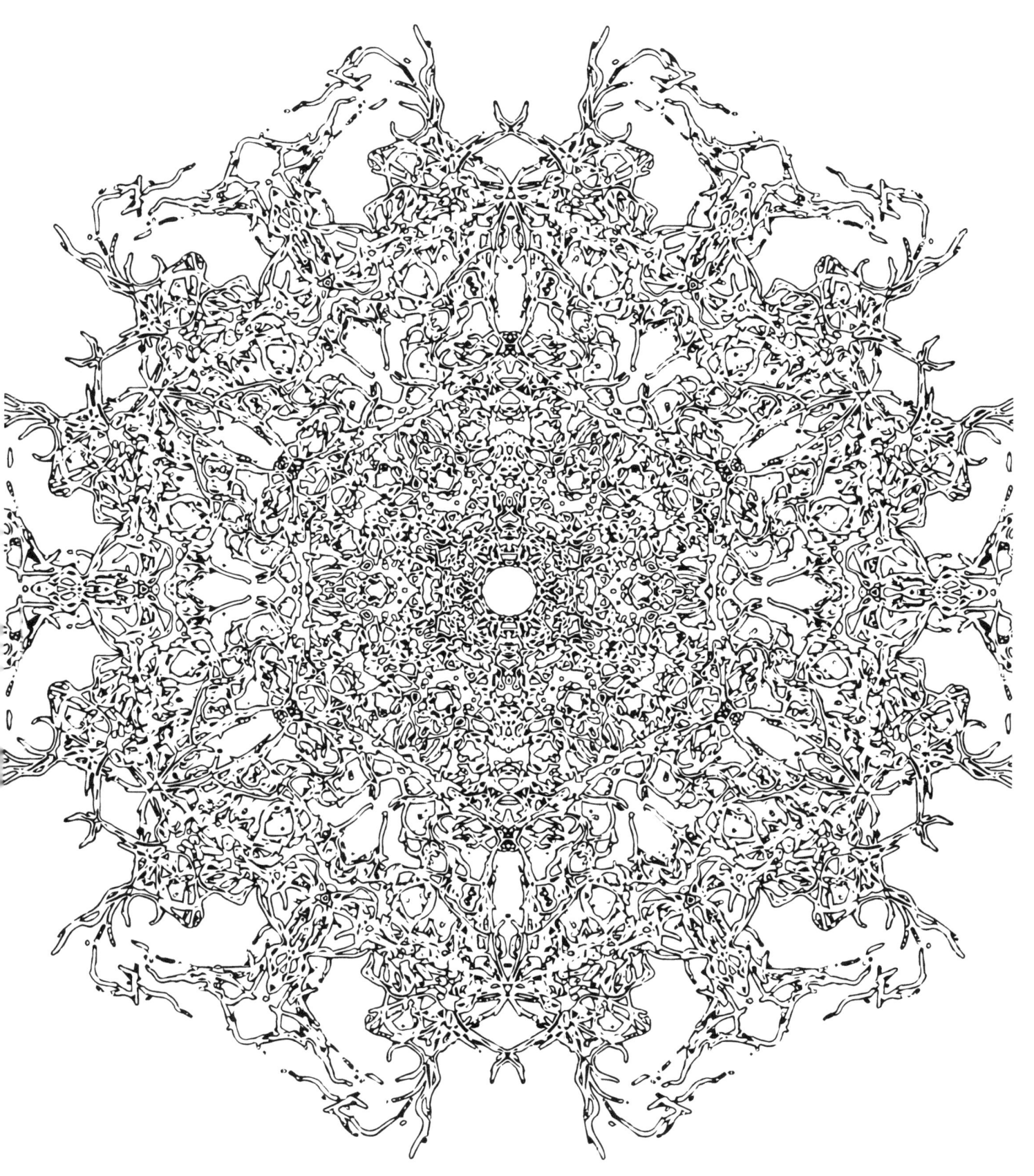

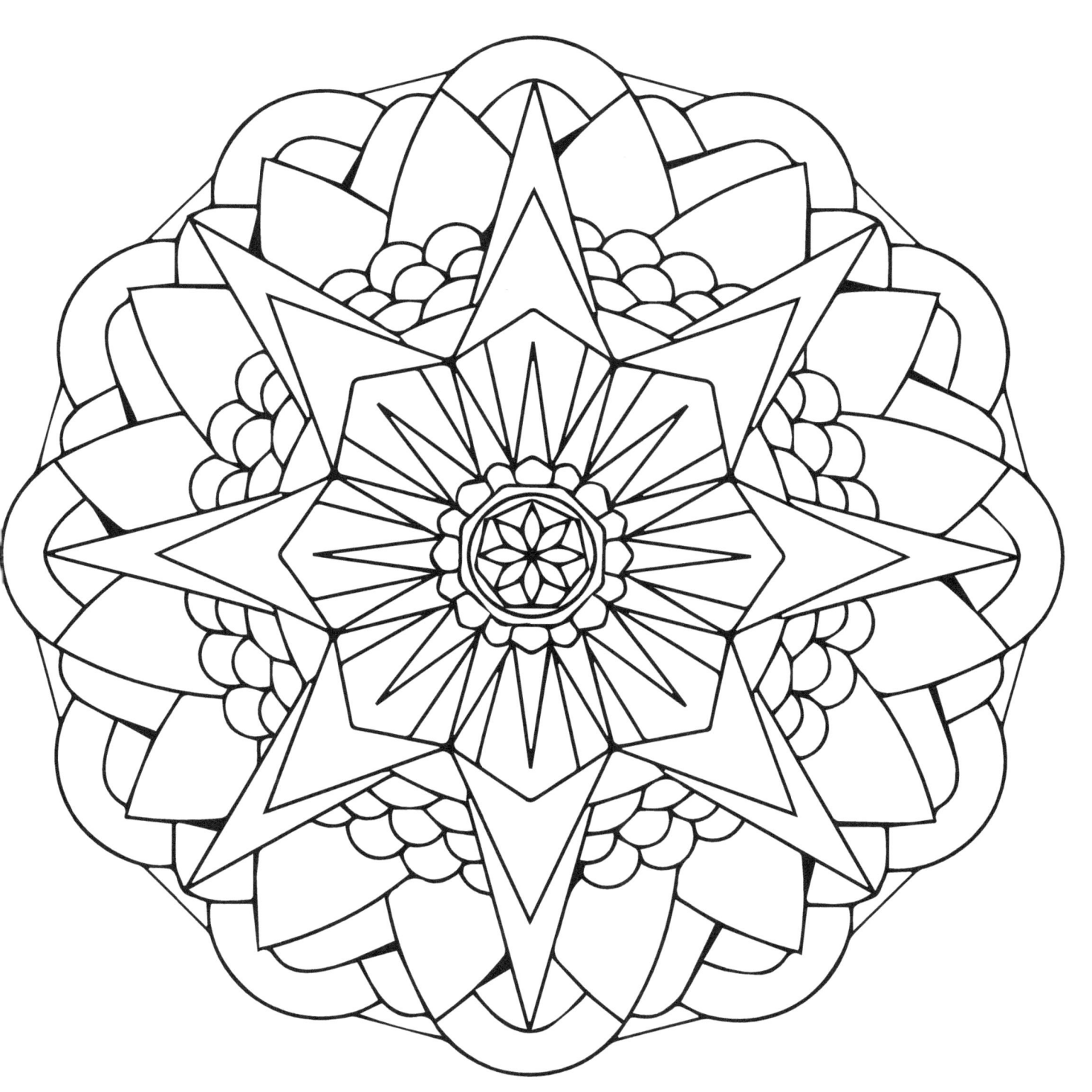

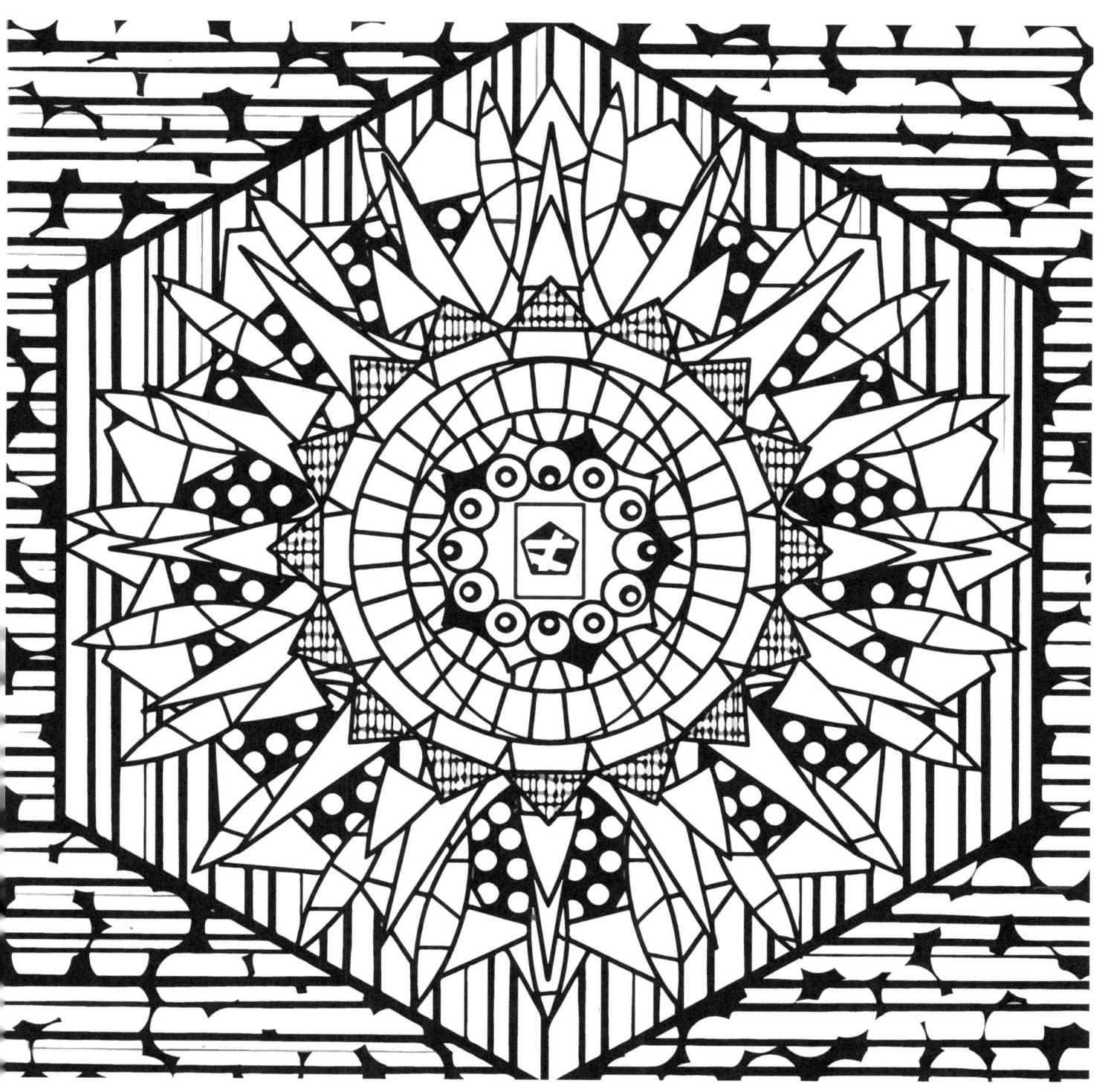

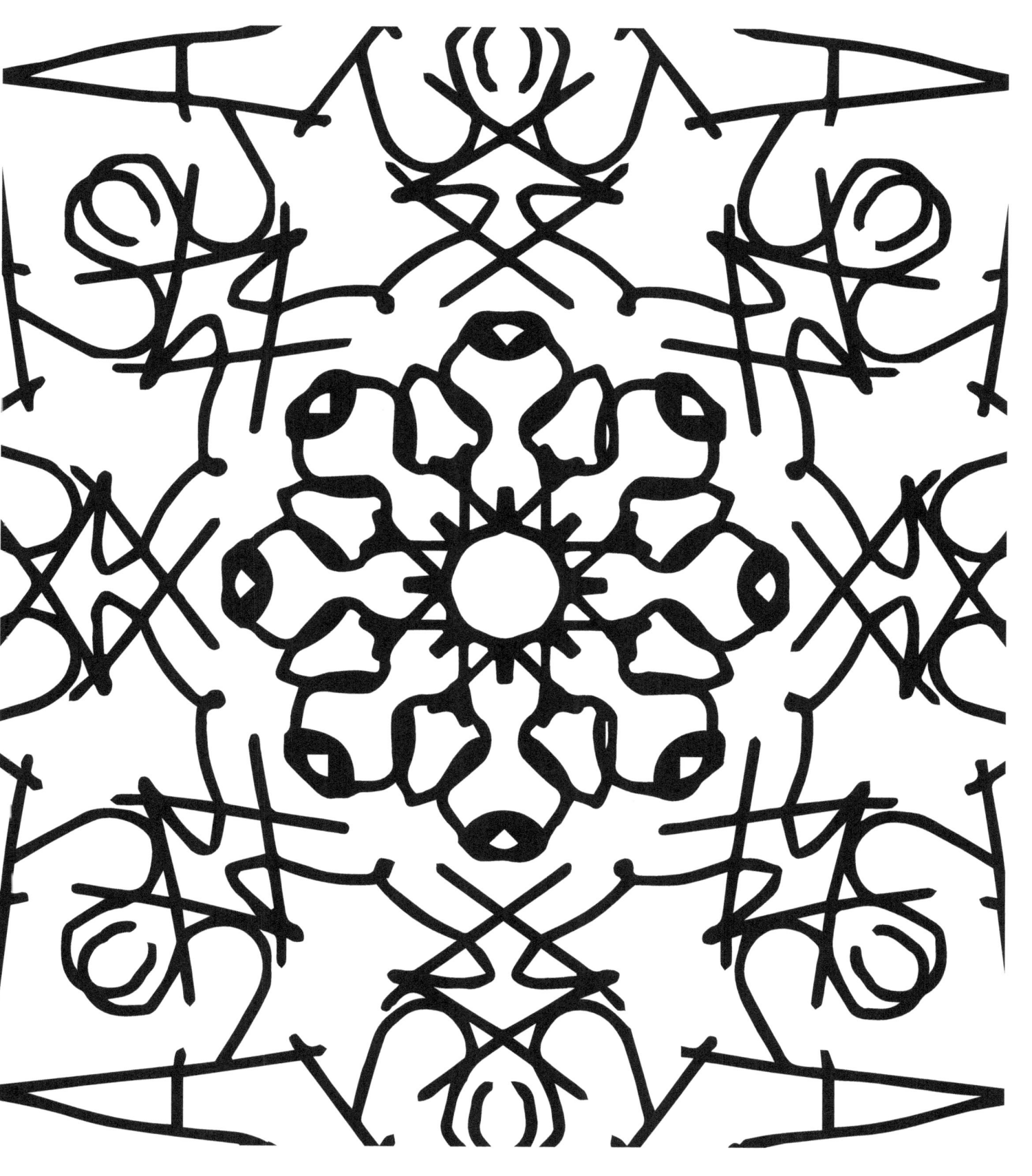

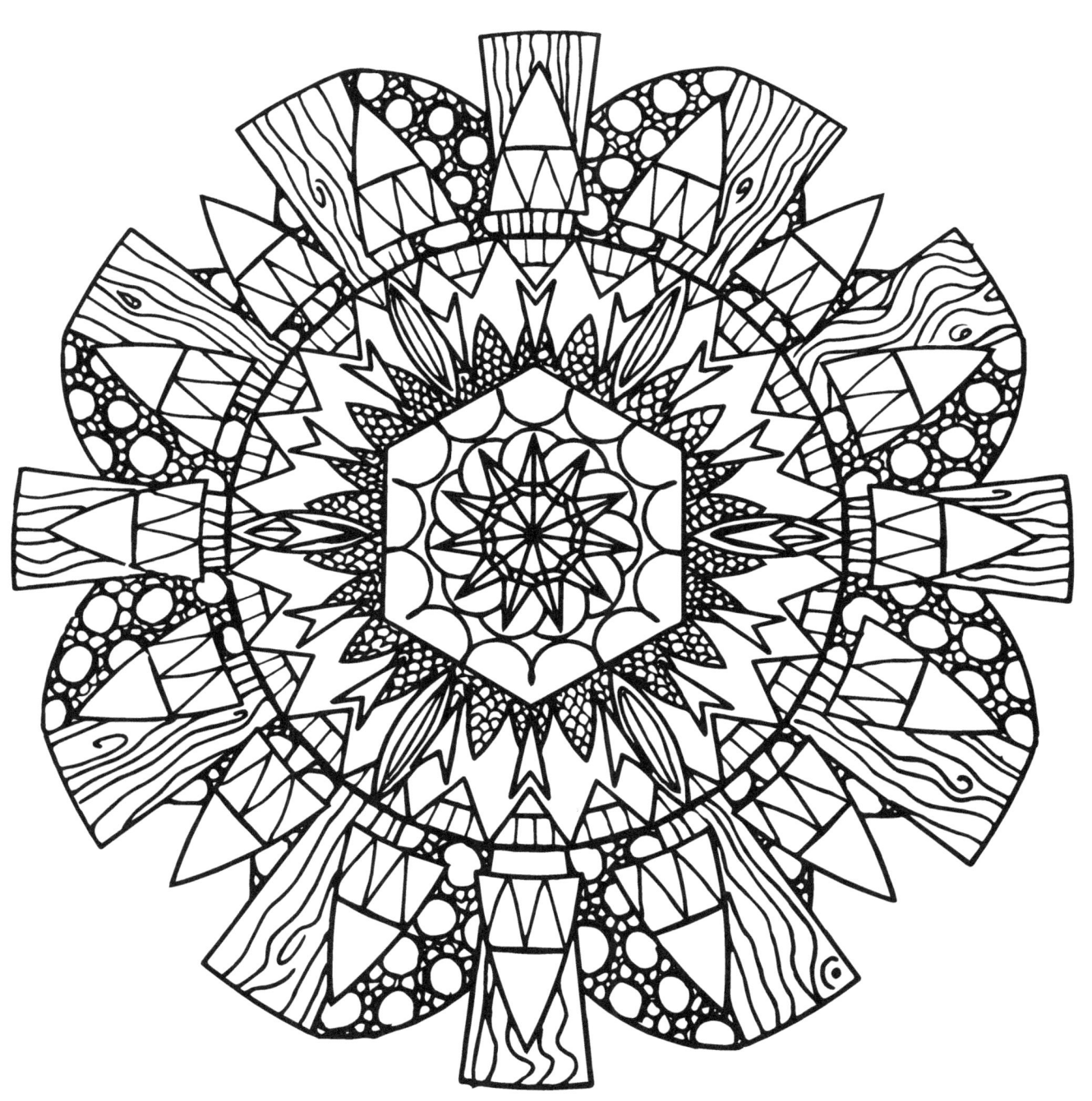

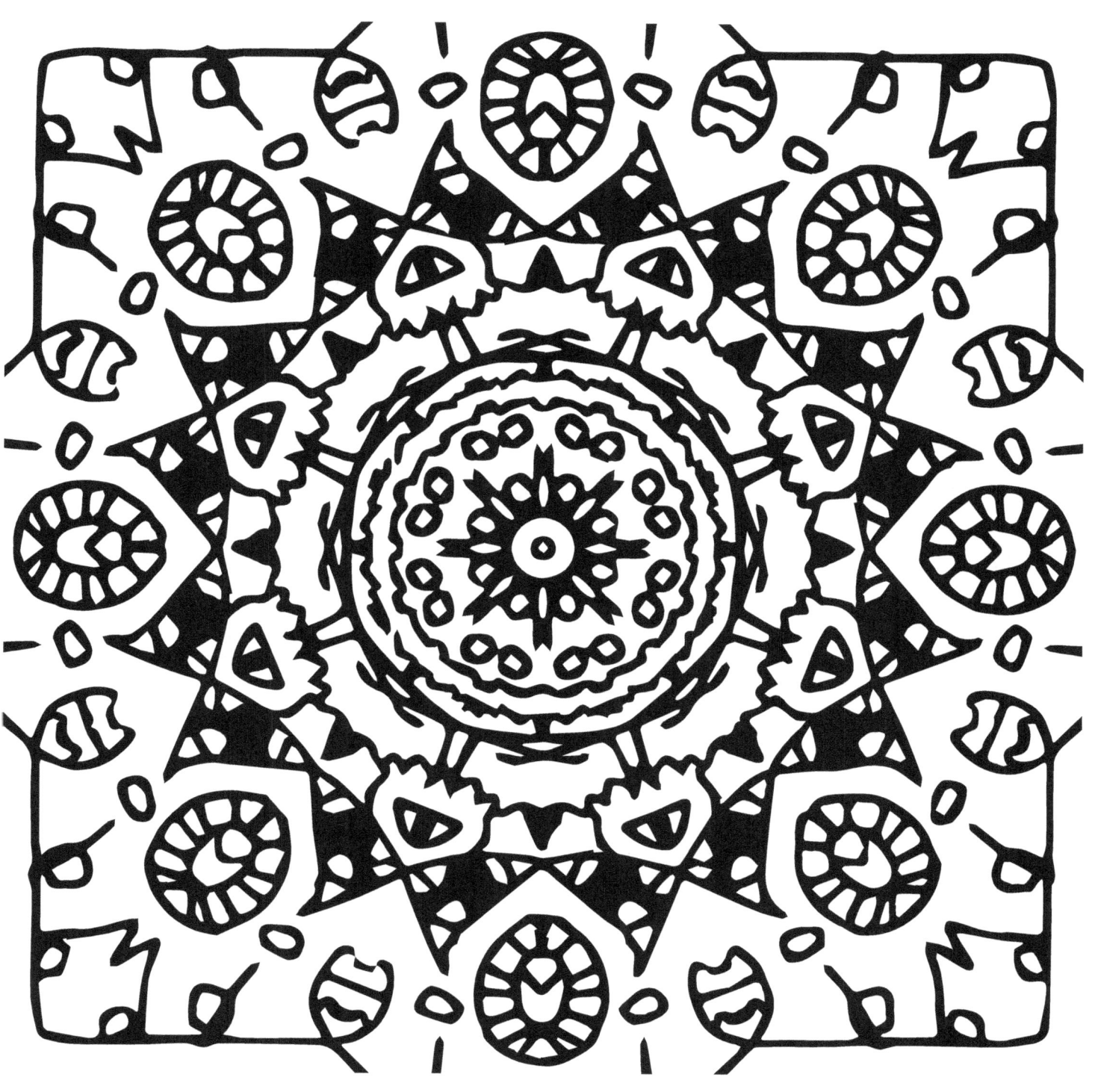

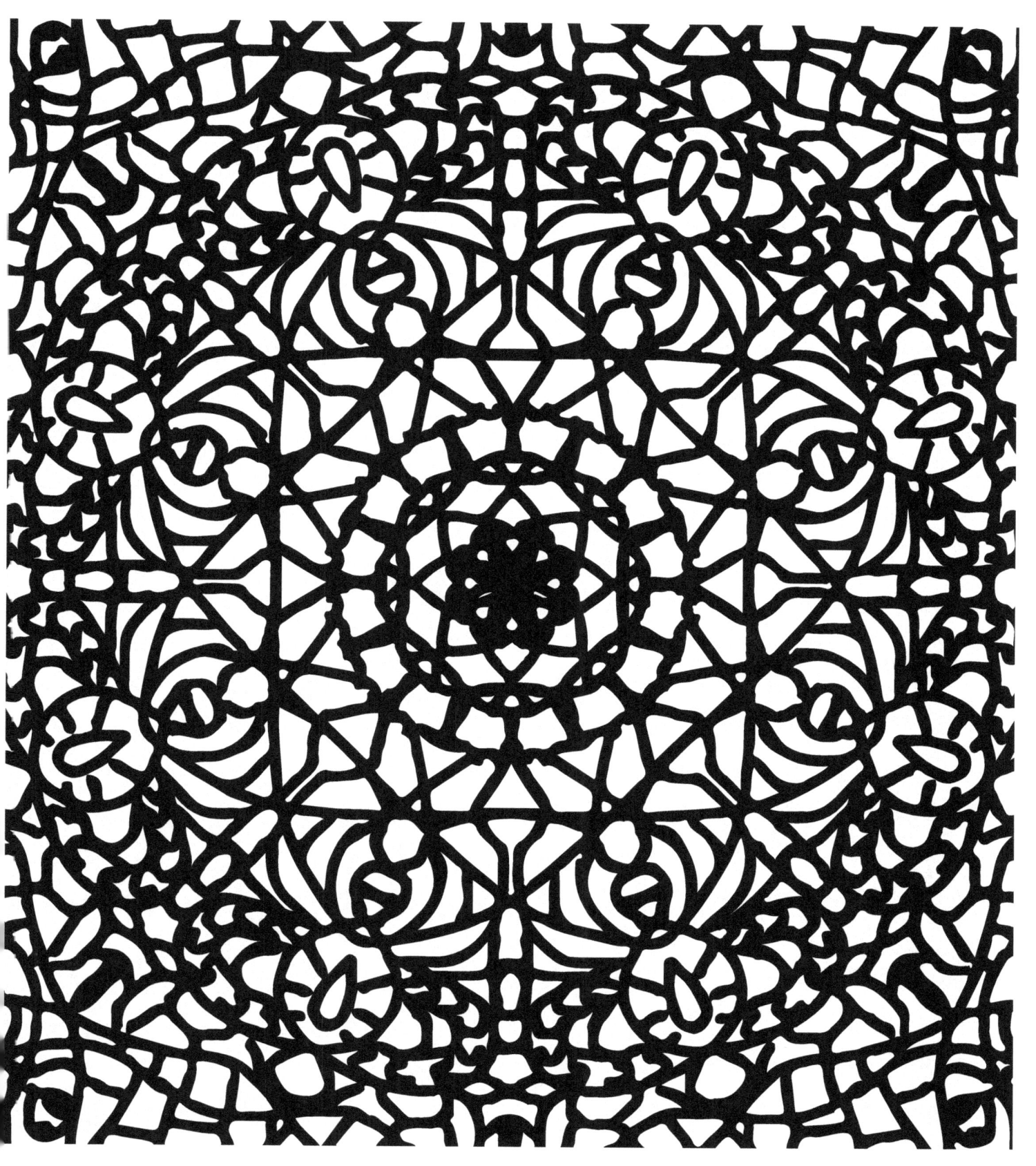

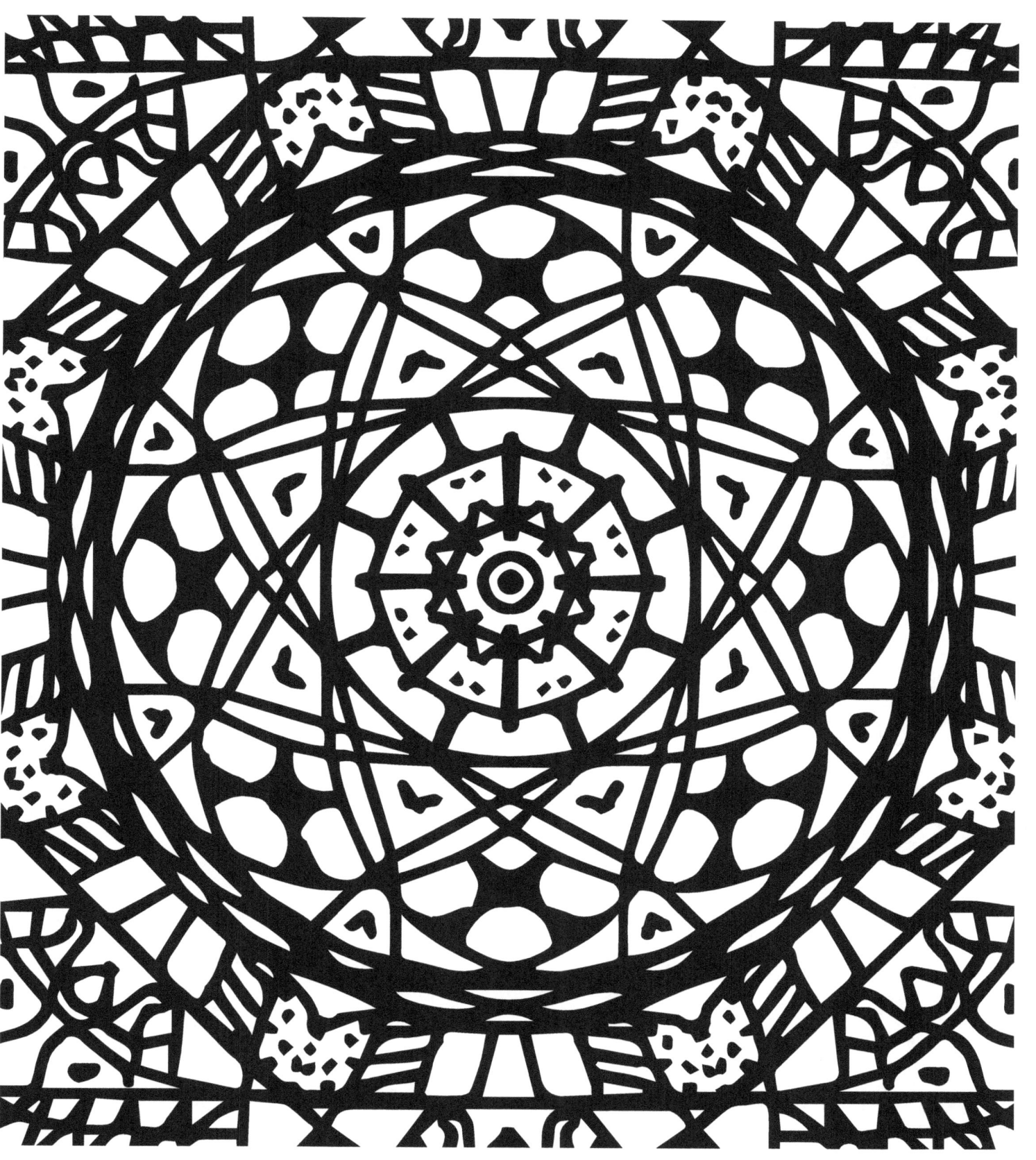

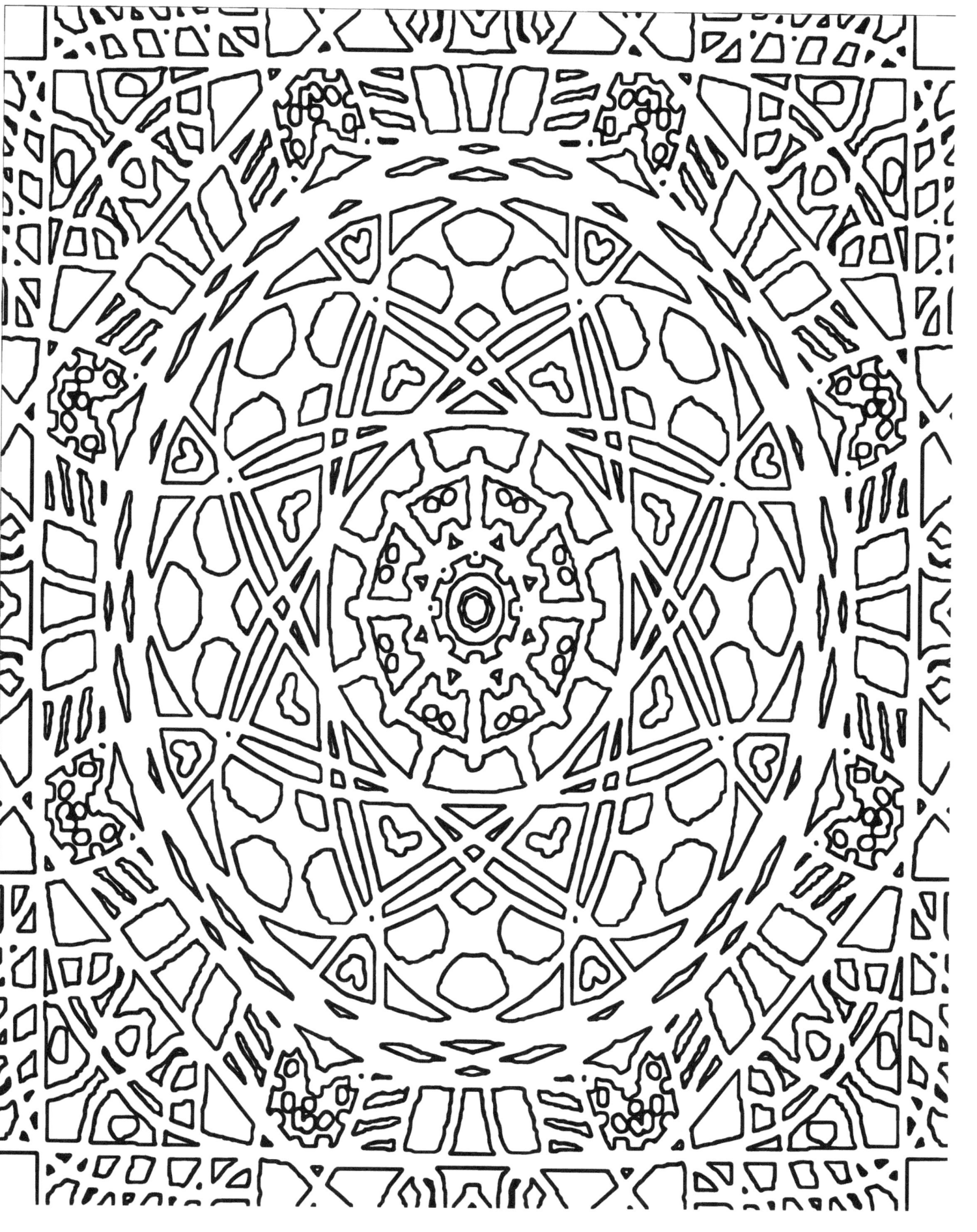

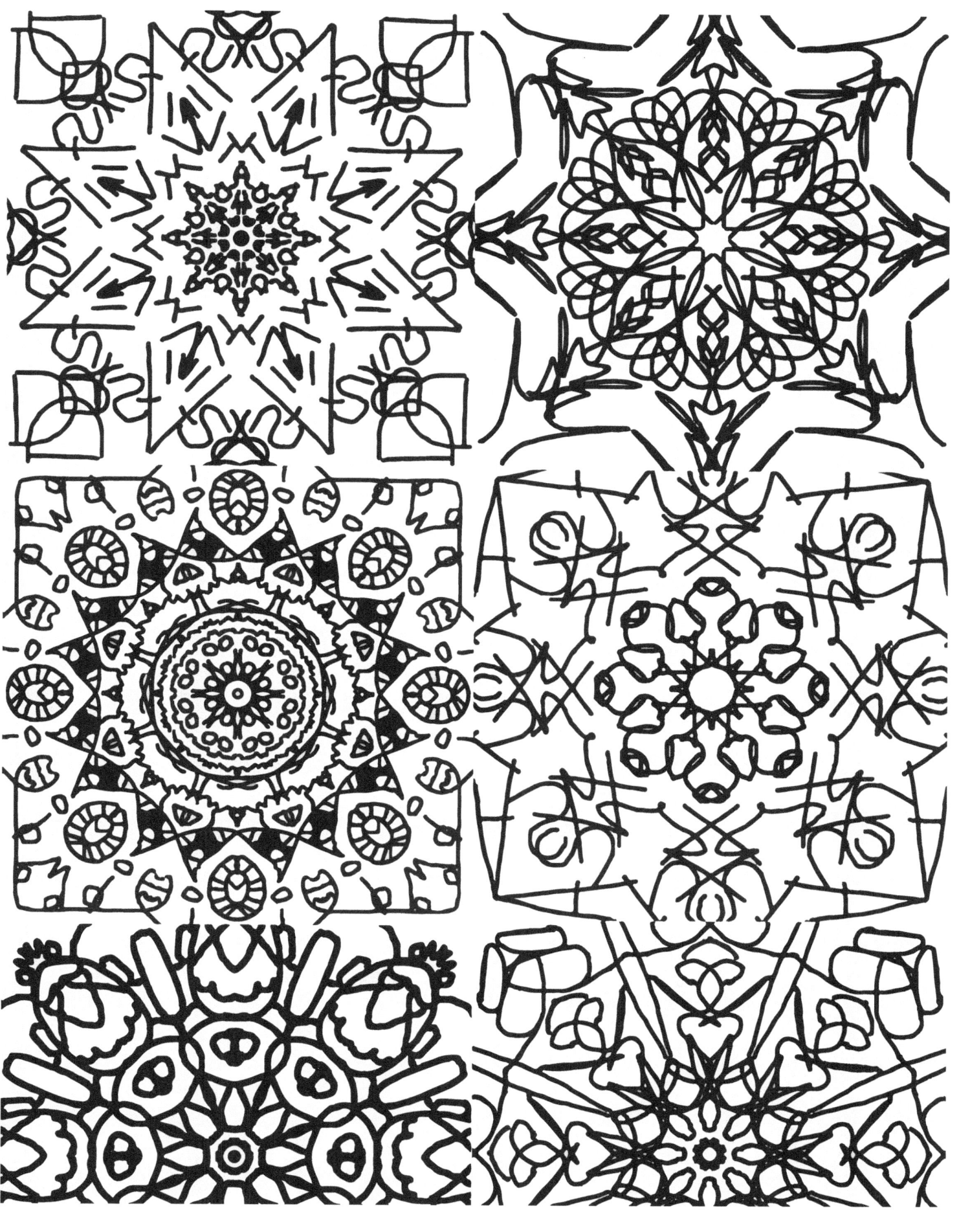

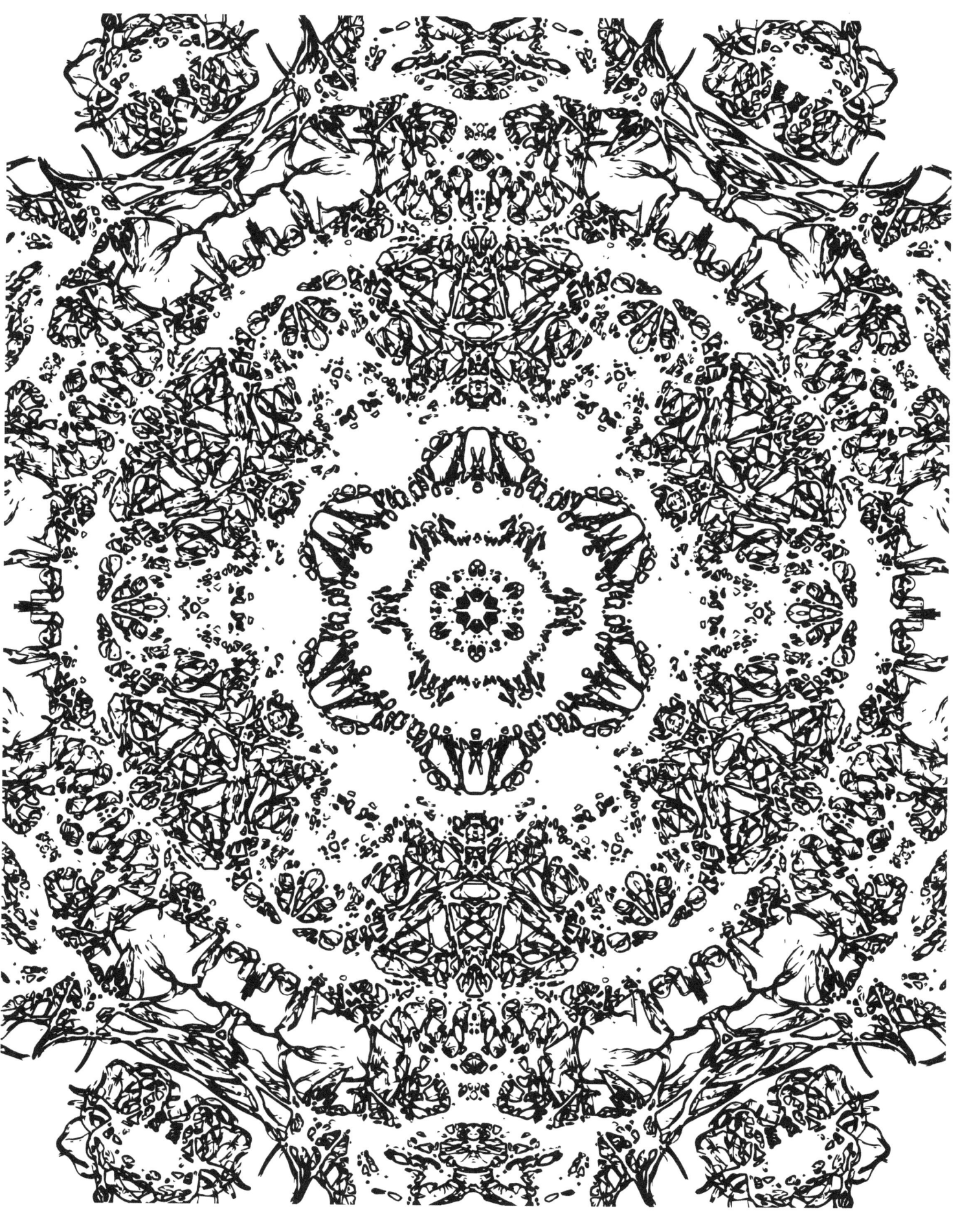

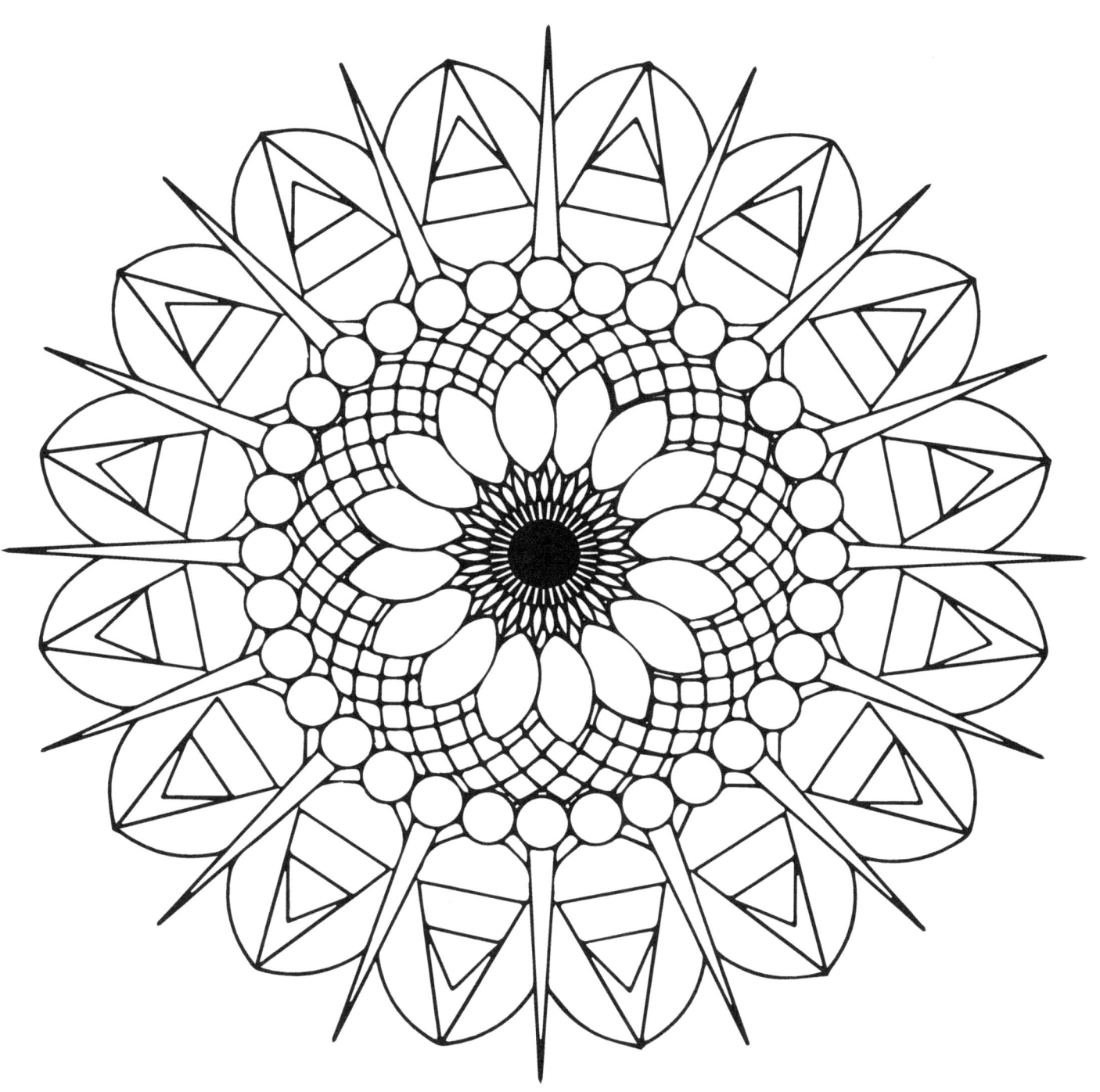

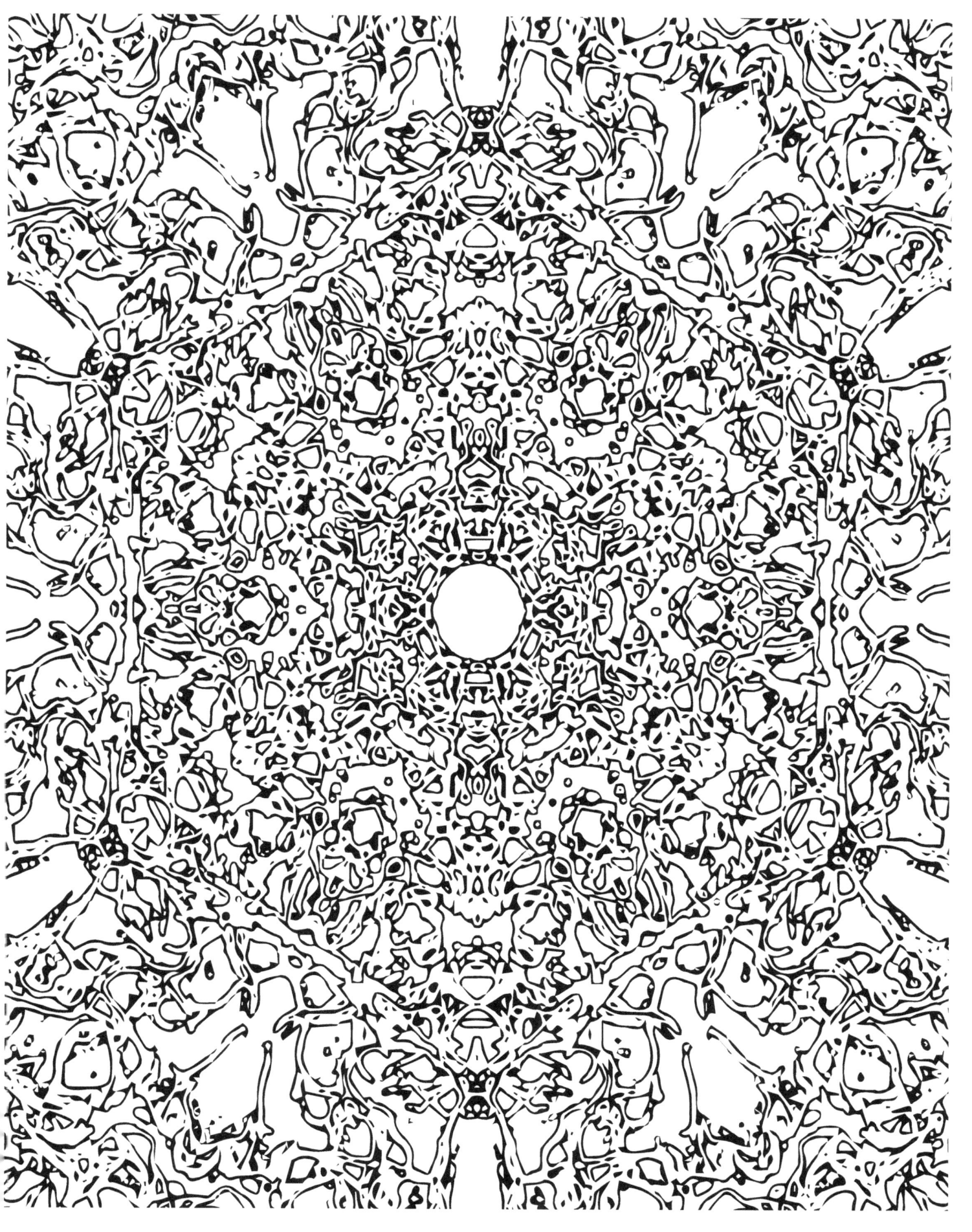

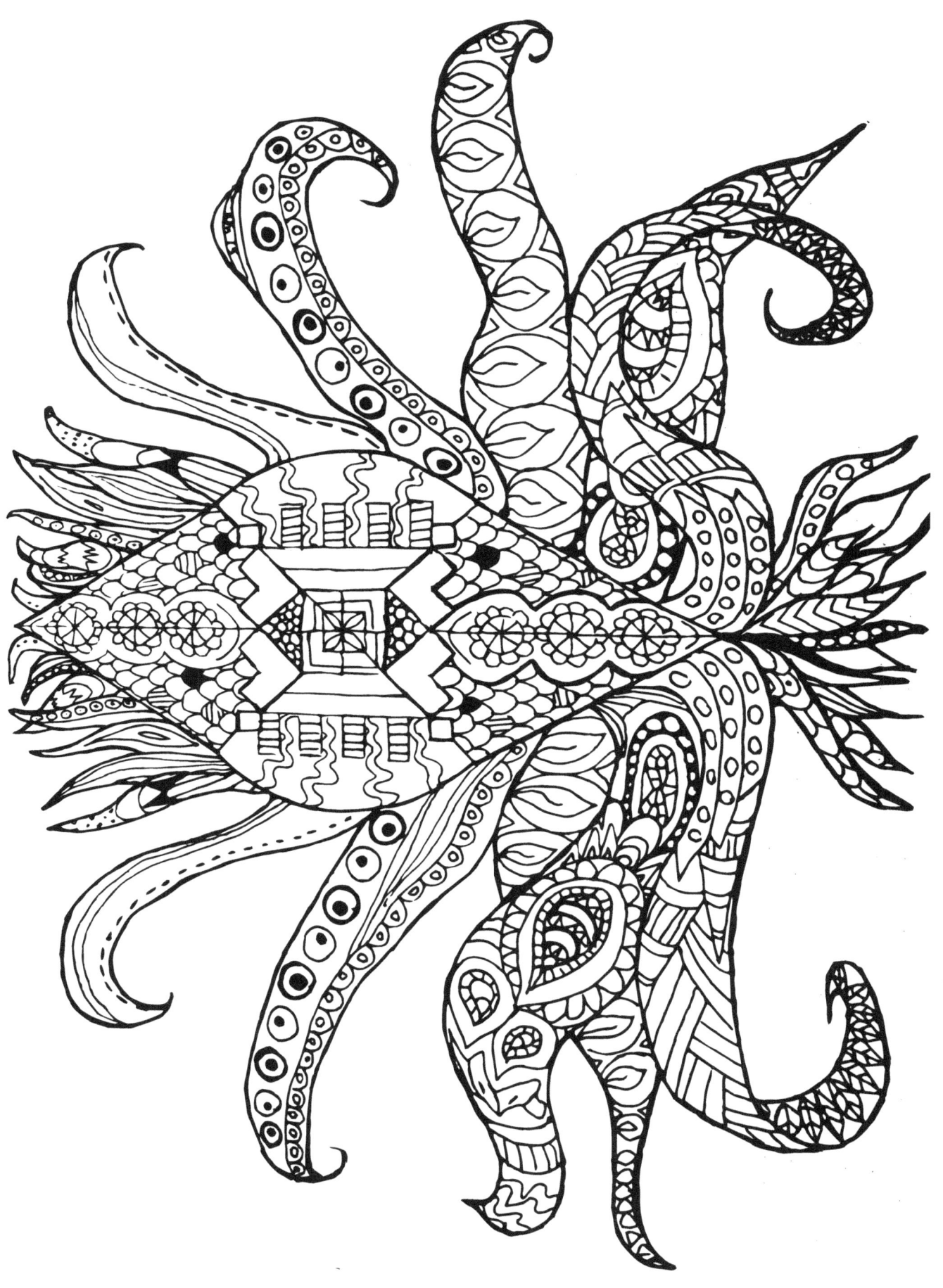

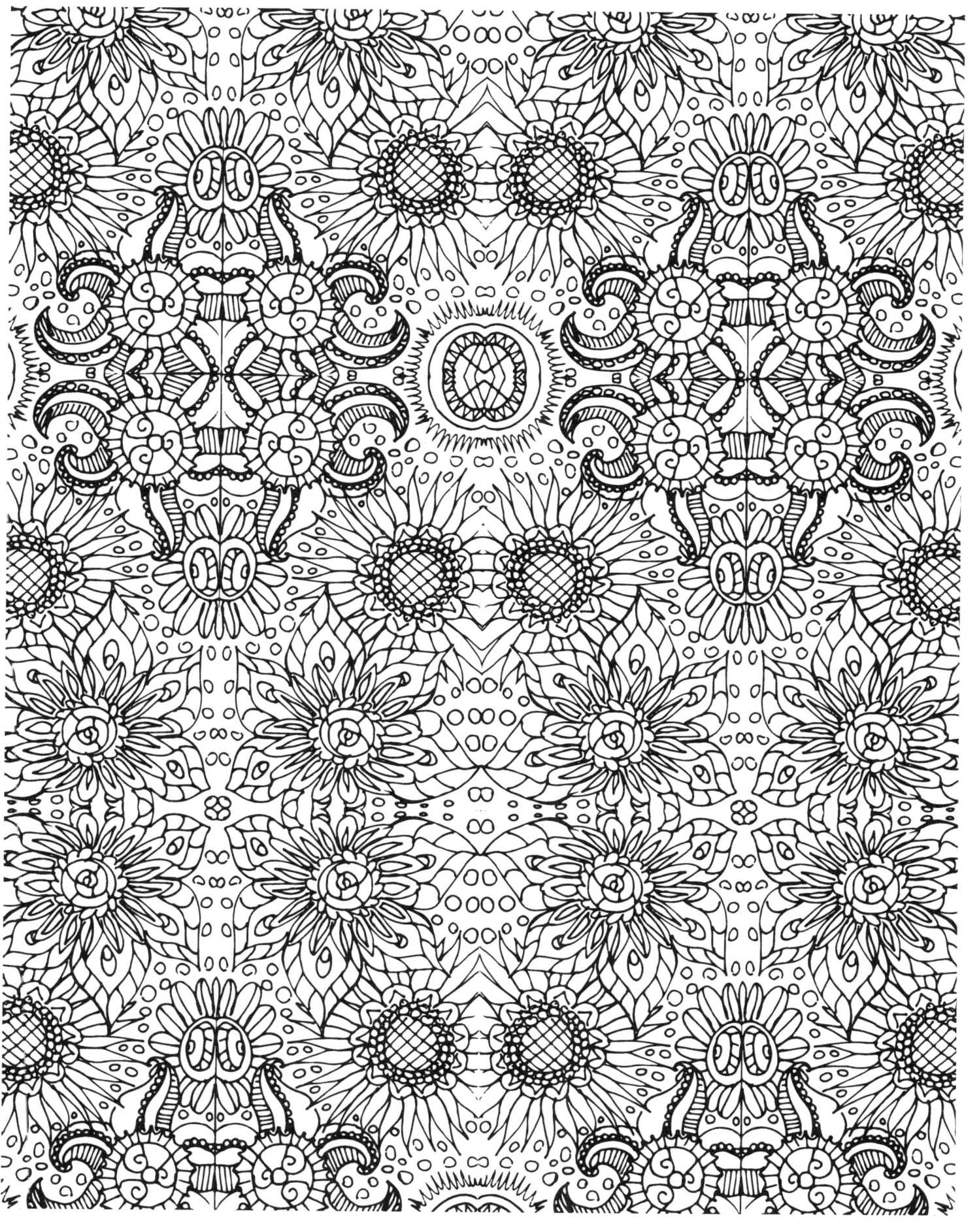

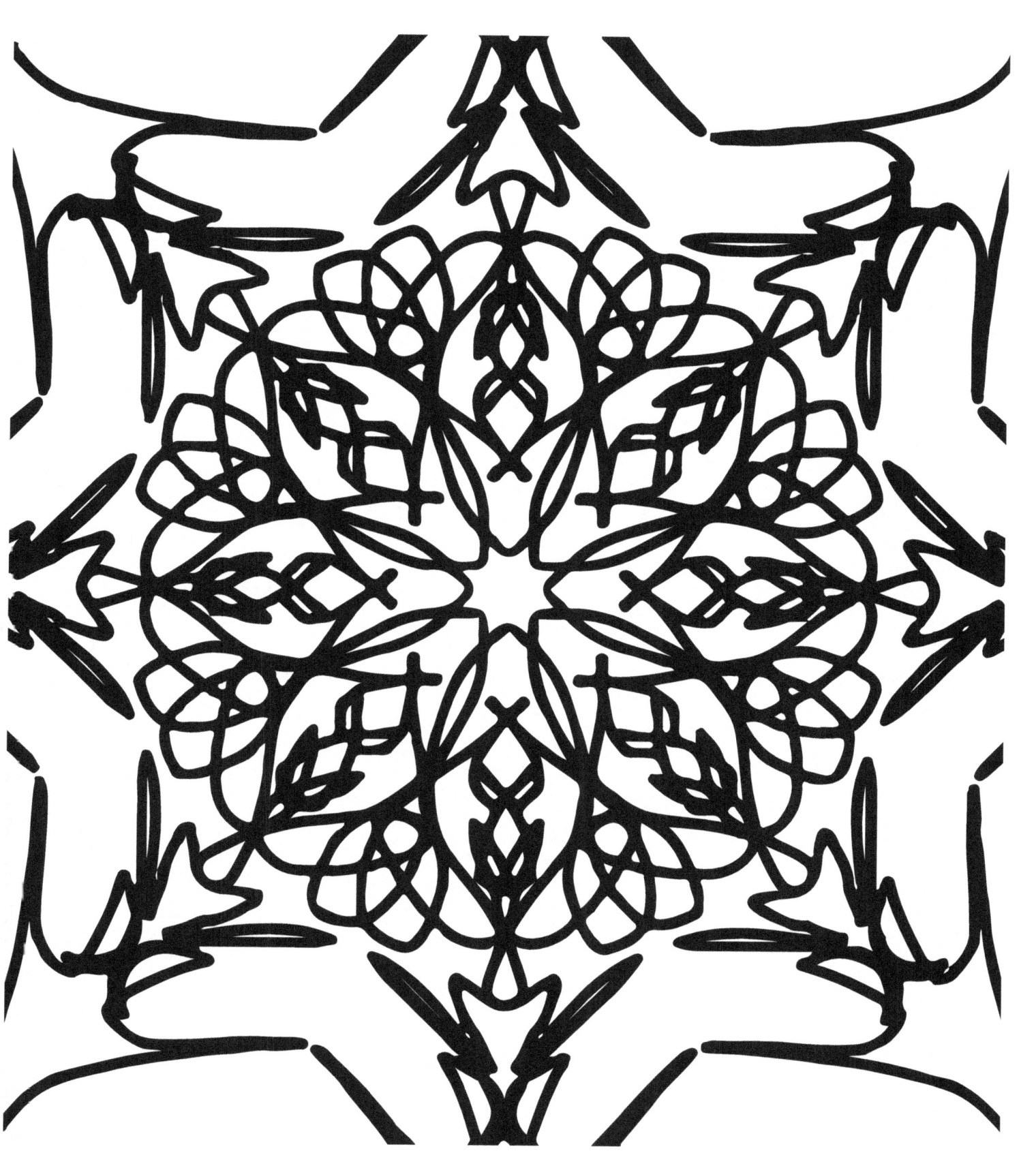

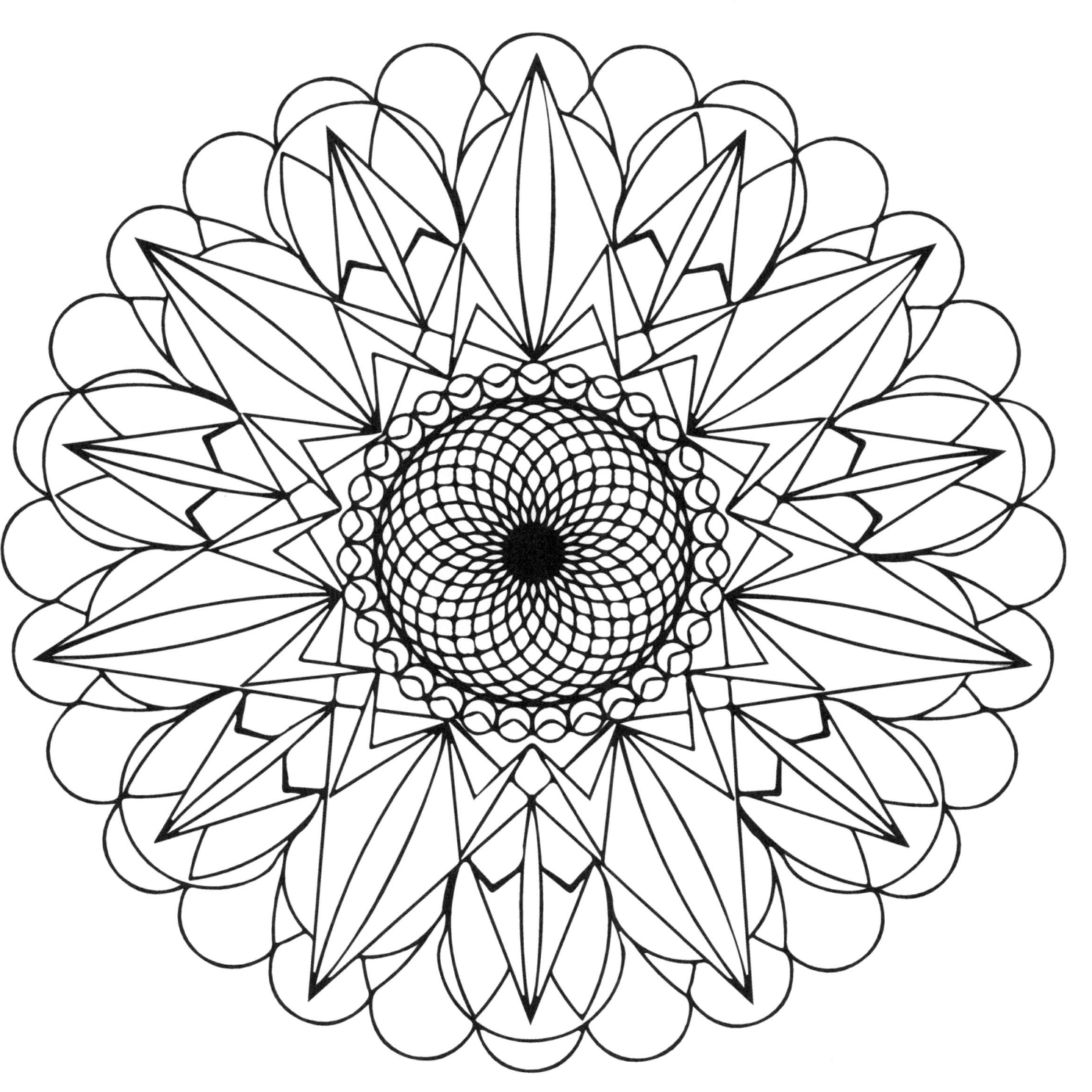

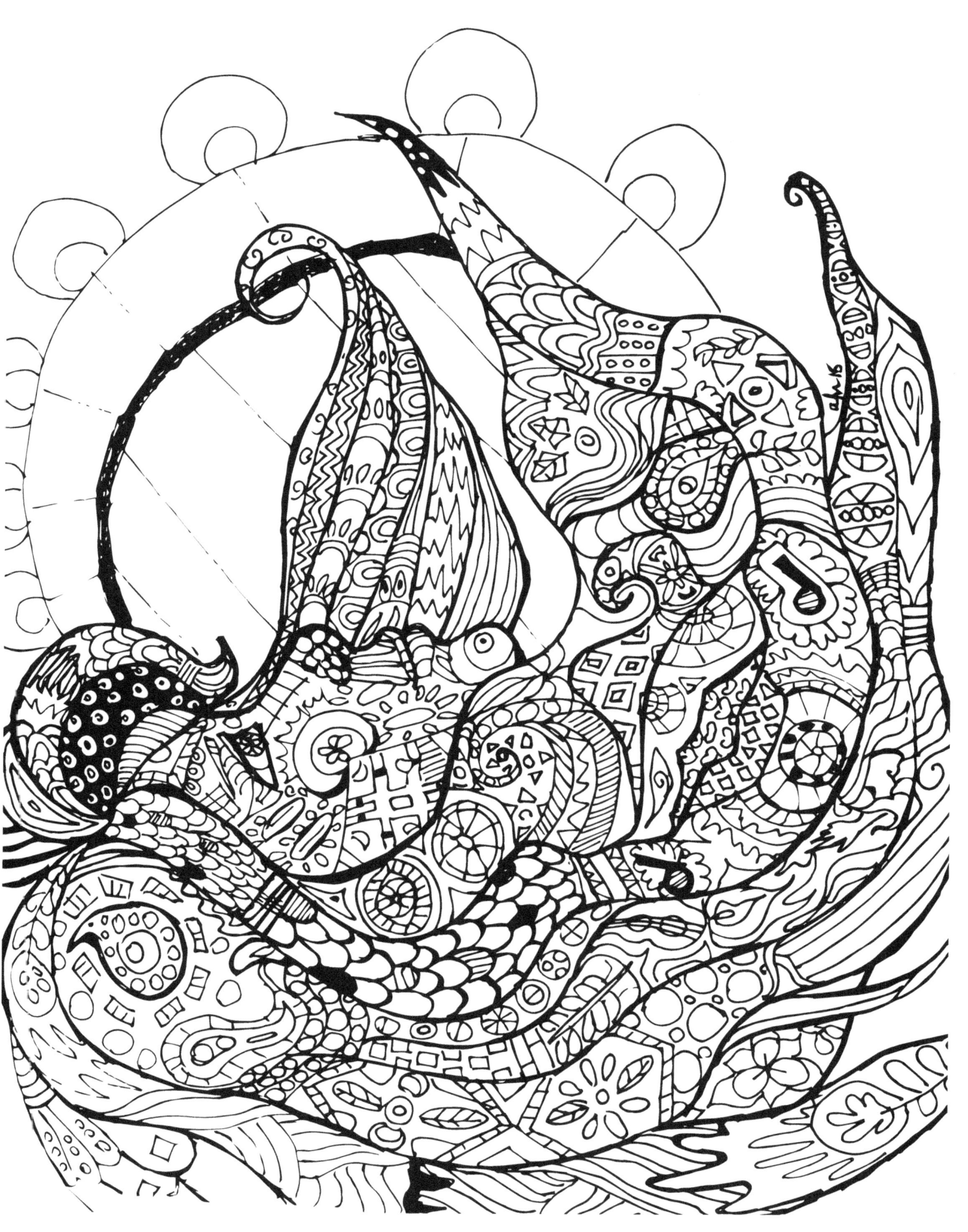

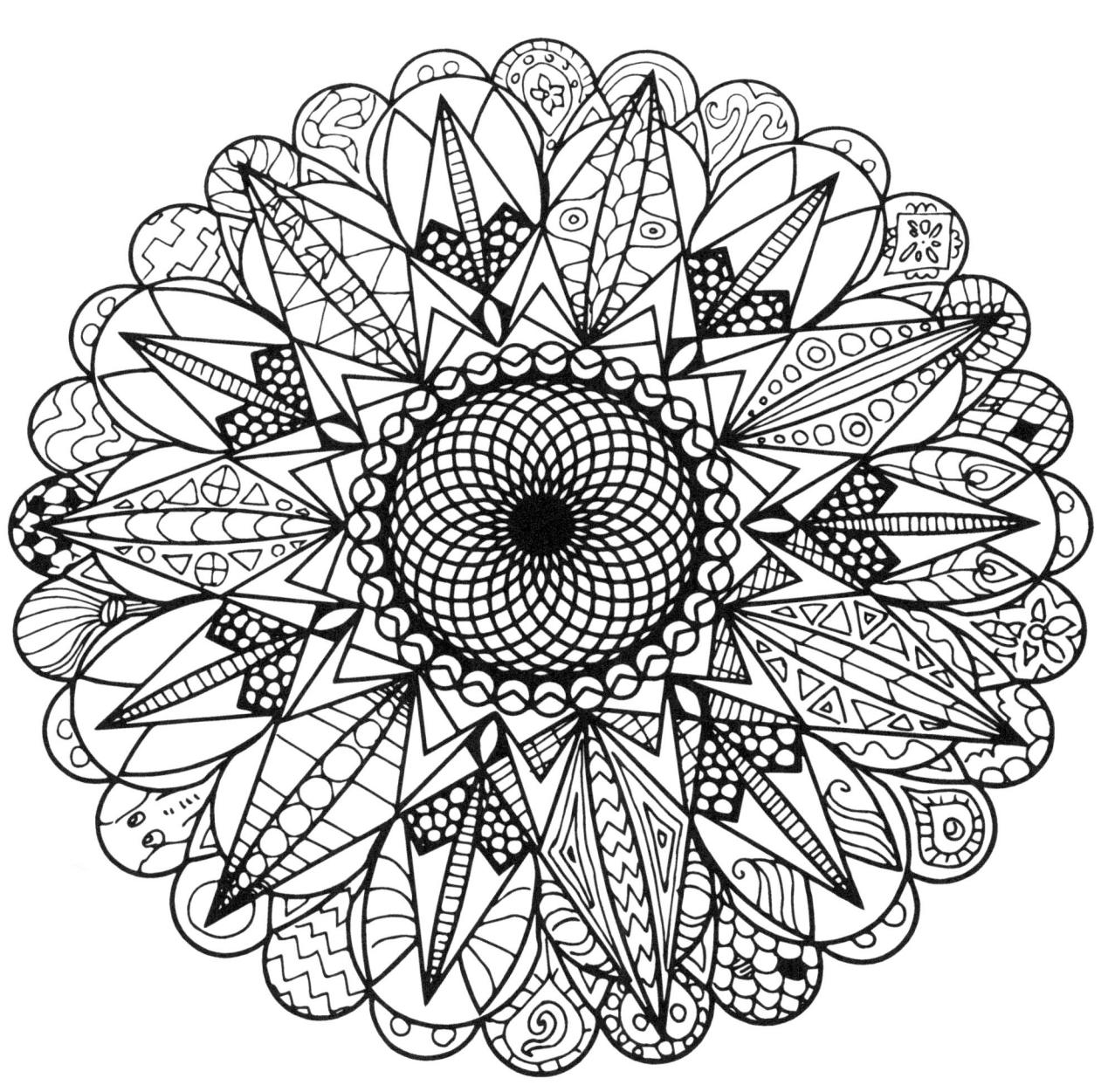

www.ingramcontent.com/pod-product-compliance
Lightning Source LLC
Chambersburg PA
CBHW080615180526
45168CB00007B/2919